SCIENTOLOGY
Making the World a Better Place

CW00485893

Founded and developed by L. Ron Hubbard, Scientology is an applied religious philosophy which offers an exact route through which anyone can regain the truth and simplicity of his spiritual self.

Scientology consists of specific axioms that define the underlying causes and principles of existence and a vast area of observations in the humanities, a philosophic body that literally applies to the entirety of life.

This broad body of knowledge resulted in two applications of the subject: first, a technology for man to increase his spiritual awareness and attain the freedom sought by many great philosophic teachings; and, second, a great number of fundamental principles men can use to improve their lives. In fact, in this second application, Scientology offers nothing less than practical methods to better *every* aspect of our existence—means to create new ways of life. And from this comes the subject matter you are about to read.

Compiled from the writings of L. Ron Hubbard, the data presented here is but one of the tools which can be found in *The Scientology Handbook*. A comprehensive guide, the handbook contains numerous applications of Scientology which can be used to improve many other areas of life.

In this booklet, the editors have augmented the data with a short introduction, practical exercises and examples of successful application.

Courses to increase your understanding and further materials to broaden your knowledge are available at your nearest Scientology church or mission, listed at the back of this booklet.

Many new phenomena about man and life are described in Scientology, and so you may encounter terms in these pages you are not familiar with. These are described the first time they appear and in the glossary at the back of the booklet.

Scientology is for use. It is a practical philosophy, something one *does*. Using this data, you *can* change conditions.

Millions of people who want to do something about the conditions they see around them have applied this knowledge. They know that life can be improved. And they know that Scientology works.

Use what you read in these pages to help yourself and others and you will too.

CHURCH OF SCIENTOLOGY INTERNATIONAL

*A*nybody *recognizes that if things were better organized people would be better off. We have all had experiences with bureaucratic red tape, impersonal government agencies or careless commercial enterprises. The problem of poor organization is serious and costs trillions in waste, inefficiency and lowered productivity.*

On a more individual level, organization is a key—and often missing—factor in personal success. It is also a necessity for a flourishing family. Attainment of one's goals, no matter how small or how large, requires a knowledge of organization. How do you most efficiently and productively manage your time, your activities and your resources? How do you minimize distractions? And how do you align your strengths in order to accomplish your purposes?

L. Ron Hubbard recognized that man was as lacking in understanding of how to organize his activities as he was about his true spiritual nature. And a sizable portion of his research was devoted to clarify the subject of organization, a task he fully accomplished.

This booklet contains only some of the most basic principles of the organizing technology he developed, but these fundamentals are, by themselves, enough to greatly enhance the activity of any endeavor, whether that of a group or an individual. Chaos and confusion are not natural conditions of life.

They only exist when natural laws are not understood and followed. Here are some of the natural laws of organization and organizing.■

ORGANIZATION

I t may be that in trying to get something going, the basic of organization may be missing.

The word *organize* means to form into a whole with mutually connected and dependent parts; to give a definite and orderly structure to. From this, one gets the term *organization.*

Organization is the subdivision of actions and duties into specialized functions.

One can organize a series of actions to be done by himself or herself. This would consist of seeing what has to be done, doing what one can do first and then the remainder as a feasible series of events, all to accomplish a final completion of an action which forwards one's assigned or postulated purposes.

A group is organized so as to permit flows and accomplish specialized actions which are completed in themselves and from which small actions or completions the group purpose, assigned or specialized, is forwarded or accomplished.

There is a difference between directing and doing, which some people have trouble separating apart. A person in charge of an activity is sometimes found deficient in organizational understanding and so tries to do all the actions himself. This, if done to excess, effectively can break up a group and render it useless since all members but one have no function, having been robbed by this one-man monopoly on action.

True, an active and competent person *can* do things better. But he can really never do more than he can do. Whereas a well-organized group, each with specialized functions, coordinated by the in-charge, can accomplish many times the work only one can do.

Because it is *organized* makes a group harder to defeat than the individual.

A competent individual who has been let down too often by groups tends to take it all on himself rather than whip the group into shape and get things organized.

The correct action when faced by urgent necessity arising from incompetence of a group or other causes is to:

1. Handle it,

2. Organize the group to handle such things and do their jobs.

One can get stuck on (1) and, if he or she does, then will have trouble and overwork from there on out. Because he or she omits *also* doing (2).

The major failure of any group is to fail to organize.

Workers of the world may arise, but if they are not quickly organized before or after the fact, they will promptly be put back down!

The major cause of not organizing is just not understanding what is meant by it.

For example, an executive is told he is in charge of seeing that the X project is done. He doesn't know much about it. He has two men who do know. The incorrect action is to try to do the X project himself or issue a lot of unreal orders about it. The correct action is to call up the man who does know, give him the other as an assistant and tell them to get on with it. Then, without interfering, the executive who received the order should get more knowledgeable about the X project so *he* can be sure it is done, while still letting the designated people get on with it.

This comprehension of organization is as simple as this—put somebody on the job and let him get on with it. On a project, make a survey of all the things there are to do, group types of actions into single jobs, assign people to them, provide the routes on which communications travel between group members, materiel and liaison and let the group get on with it.

Any job, no matter how junior, has to be organized.

Anyone in charge of people has to be able to organize functions and work.

Failing that, one gets very little done and is badly overworked. And the rest of the group is wasted.

By understanding that there is a subject called organization, that the subject has been codified and that it can be learned and applied, any individual or group can succeed in its endeavors.

BASIC ORGANIZATION

What is organization?

Most people have so many associated ideas with the word "organization" that they think of one as an identity or a being, not as a dynamic activity.

Let's see what one really is.

Let us take a pile of red, white and blue beads. Let's organize them.

Now let us draw the org board. In brief, an *org board* (short for *organizing board*) shows the functions, duties, communication routes, sequences of actions and authorities of an organization.

Let us dump the beads all on top of in-charge, all mixed up in a confusion.

Obviously in-charge must *route* them to dig himself out. So we get:

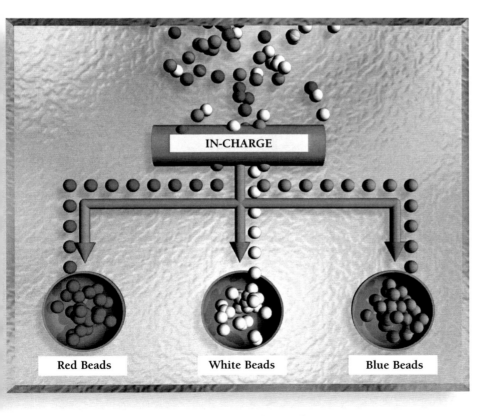

Thus we find out much of what an in-charge does. He routes. He separates into types or classes of thing or action.

This so far is a motionless organization.

We have to have products. By *product* we mean a completed thing that has exchange value within or outside the activity. This can be a service or article that has been put into the hands of someone outside the organization or another member of the organization.

Let's say the organization's products are drilled beads, strung beads, boxed beads.

We would get:

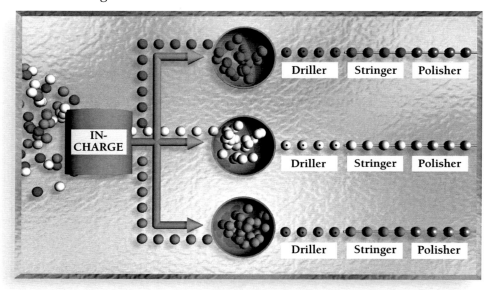

Or we would get:

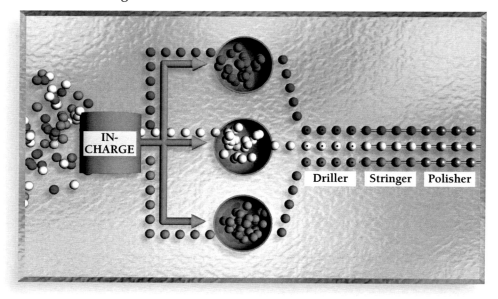

Or we would get:

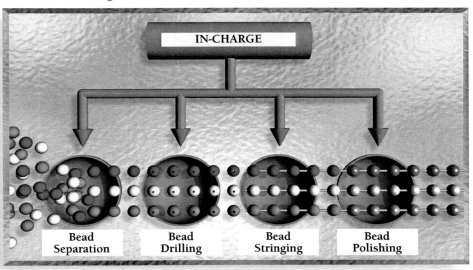

It is not particularly important which pattern of org board we use so long as it handles the volume of beads.

If we only have one person in this "organization," he would still have to have some idea of organization and a sort of org board.

If we have any volume to handle we have to add people. If we add them without an org board we will also add confusion. The organization without an org board will break down by overload and cross flows and currents. These in conflict become confusion.

All a confusion is, is unpatterned flow of particles (bodies, communications or other items). The particles collide, bounce off each other and stay IN the area. Thus there is no product, as to have a *product* something must flow OUT.

We can now note two things. We have some stable items. These are locations or posts (jobs, positions in a group or organization). And we have flow items. These are things undergoing change.

So an organization's positions change flowing particles.

Particles flow *in sequence.*

Things enter an organization, get changed, flow out of an organization.

An organization with one type of item only (red beads) is less complex than one with several types of items.

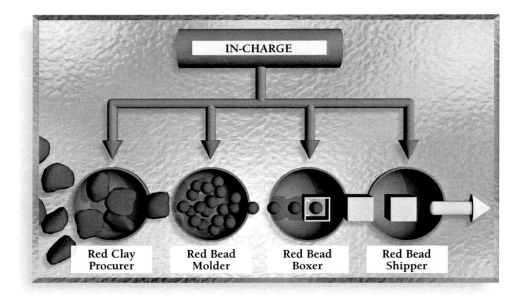

Any activity has a *sequence* of actions. It has to have stable points which do *not* flow in order to handle things which do flow.

It is not necessary to have a stable terminal do only one thing. But if so then it also has a correct sequence of actions. (By "terminal" is meant a person who sends, receives or relays communication.)

All this is true of an engine room or a lawyer's office or any organization.

In an engine room fuel flows in and is changed to motion which flows out. Somebody runs the machines. Somebody repairs the machines. It may all be done by one person but as soon as volume goes up one has to plan out the actions, classify them and put them on an org board which the people there know and abide by, or the place will not operate well.

This is done by dividing operation and repair into two actions, making two activities on the same org board.

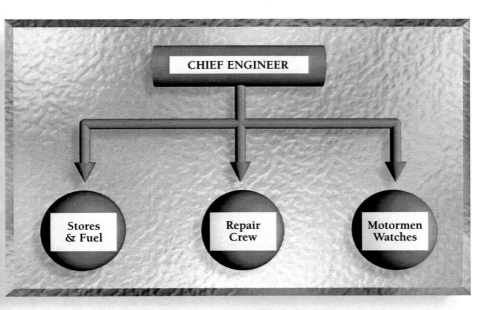

The Chief keeps the flows going and the terminals performing their actions.

In a lawyer's office we get different actions as a flow.

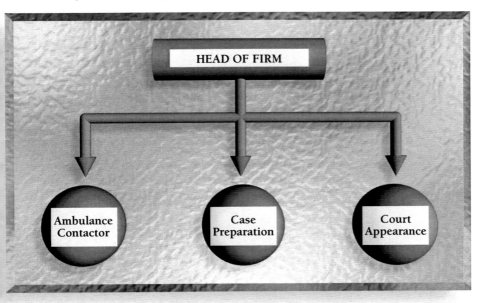

The above would be a flow pattern, possibly with a different person (with a different skill) on each point.

Or we could have a sort of motionless org board.

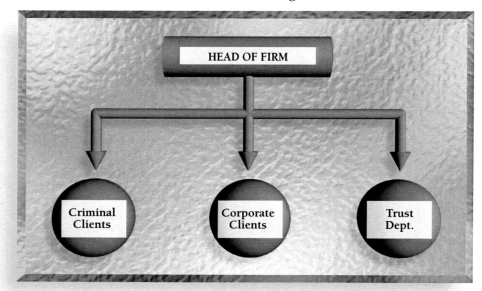

But if we did that we would have to put the motion in vertically so that flow would occur.

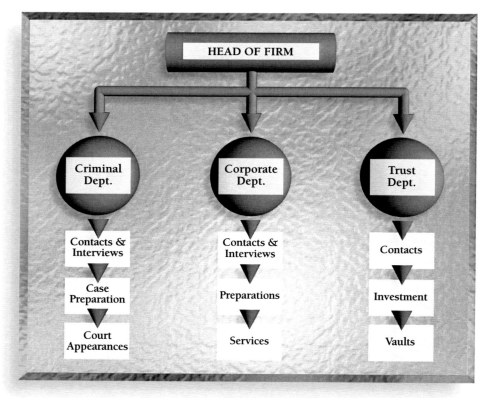

Organizing boards which only give terminals usually will not flow.

A typical army org board of yesteryear was:

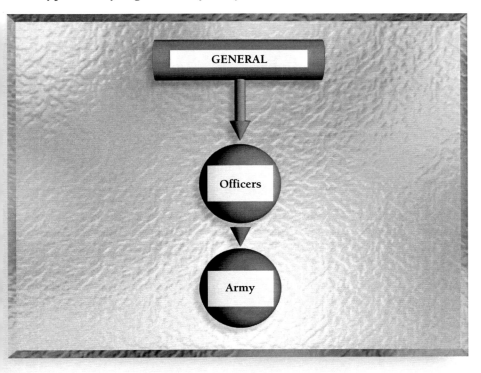

When they got into a lot more men they had to have a *flow* board.

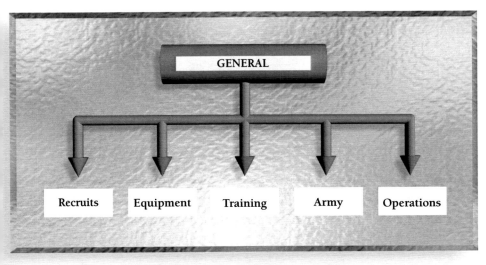

So one *organizes* by:

1. Surveying the types of particles.

2. Working out the changes desired for each to make a product.

3. Posting the terminals who will do the changing along the sequence of changes.

The board also must include a *recognition* of the types in (1) which *routes* the types to the *terminals* who *change* them and to a further *routing out* as *products.*

To be practical an org board must also provide for acquiring the materials, disposing of the product and being paid for the cycle of action (the steps done from start to finish that resulted in the product) and its supervision.

A company has various actions.

It is essentially a collection of small org boards combined to operate together as a large org board.

The basic principles you have to know to organize anything are contained in this section of the booklet.

To plan out *any* action one has to be able to visualize its sequence of flows and the changes that occur at each point. One has to be able to see where a particle (paper, body, money) comes in and where it leaves.

One has to be able to spot any point it will halt and mend that part of the flow or handle it.

A proper org board is a perpetual combination of flows which do not collide with one another and which do enter and do experience the desired change and which do leave as a product.

ORGANIZING AND HATS

The org board shows the pattern of organizing to obtain a product.

A board then is a flow chart of consecutive *products* brought about by terminals in series.

We see these terminals as "posts" or positions.

Each one of these is a hat.

The term *hat* is slang for the title and work of a post in an organization. It is taken from the fact that in many professions such as railroading the type of hat worn is the badge of the job. For example, a train crew has a conductor who wears a conductor's hat—he has charge of the passengers and collects fares.

In an organization, there is a flow along these hats.

The result of the whole board is a product.

The product of each hat on the board adds up to the total product.

Working It Out

The waste of people involved in no org board and the loss of product justify any amount of effort to work out, make known and use a proper org board.

Man instinctively uses an org board and protests the lack of one. The rawest recruit walking aboard a ship assumes the existence of an org board, if not a posted one, at least a known one. He assumes there will be somebody in charge and that different activities will be under different people. When there is no known org board he protests. He also feels insecure as he doesn't know where he fits into this organization.

Almost all revolts are manned by people who have been excluded out and are not on the country's org board. This is so true that a ridiculous circumstance occurred in the US. A president found he had "professional relief receivers." Certain people had assumed the status of "government dependent" and were giving this as their profession. It was of course a post of sorts. And because it wasn't admitted as a post by the government, there were some riots.

The effort to belong or to be part of is expressed by an org board. A person with no post is quite miserable. A person with an unreal post feels like a fraud or a mistake.

Morale then is also considerably affected by the quality of an org board or its absence.

The overall test for the group, however, is its viability, which means its ability to grow, expand, develop, etc. Viability depends on having an acceptable product. Groups which do not have an acceptable product are not likely to survive.

The volume and acceptability of a product depends in no small measure on a workable, known org board. This is true even of an individual product.

An individual or small group, to get anywhere at all, requires a very exact org board. The oddity is that the smaller the group the more vital the org board. Yet individuals and small groups are the least likely to have one. Large groups disintegrate in the absence of an org board and go nonviable in the presence of a poor one.

The quality of a product, usually blamed on individual skill only, depends to an enormous extent upon the org board. For example, one disorganized mob that was trying to make a certain product was worked to death, harassed, angry at one another and had a wholly unacceptable product at about twice the usual cost; when organized to the degree of a third, still without proper schedules, still largely untrained, they began to turn out an acceptable product at about half the effort—so even *some* organization worked.

The product volume and quality depends utterly and totally upon the org board and hats and their use. You can train individuals endlessly but unless they are operating on a workable org board they will still have a poor or small volume product.

Lack of a known and real org board can spell failure. And lack of knowledge of the *subject* of organization has to be substituted for by pure genius at every point.

Thus to make anything at all, to improve any product, sustain morale and distribute work equitably and make it count, one has to have a real and a known org board.

So how do you make one?

Hats

An org board is made up of hats.

The definition of a hat is the "beingness and doingness that attains a product." (A beingness is the assumption or choosing of a category of identity. Doingness is the act of performing some action or activity.)

Let us take a train:

The engineer wearing his engineer hat has the title of engineer. That's the beingness.

He accepts orders, watches signals and general conditions, operates levers and valves to regulate the operation of his engine and to start, change and stop. That's the doingness.

He safely and on schedule moves the train passengers and/or freight from one location to another. A moved train and load is the product.

So how do we find out there is a hat called engineer?

As people are continually accepting or viewing already existing posts, when you ask them to dream up an org board they at first may not realize that you are asking them to *invent* the correct posts.

They don't have to invent "engineer." Everybody knows "an engineer runs a train."

So if you didn't know this? You'd have to figure it out.

One would do it this way. One would have to think along these lines:

The idea comes about because of a concept that people and goods have to be moved over distances on land. Or that a new area building up has to have transport of people and goods from and to it.

Ah. This will be viable in an economic framework because people will pay to be moved and pay for their goods to be moved.

Trains do this.

So let's use trains.

Arranging finance (or by prepayment) and obtaining a franchise for a right of way, track is laid, locomotives, train cars, stations and buildings to store and repair locomotives are built.

Now it emerges that somebody has to drive the train. So somebody had better be hired to drive the train.

So there comes into view the *post* of engineer.

How do we know this? Because we have to have a *product* of moved people and goods. That was what we were trying to do in the first place.

Therefore, the engineer hat.

So supposing now we did not have any org board at all.

The engineer hat would be the only hat. So he collects fares, runs stations, fixes his engine, buys fuel, loads the cars, sells stock....

Wait a minute. If the engineer did all that the following would happen:

1. He would be exhausted.

2. His temper would be bad.

3. He would have machinery breakdowns.

4. He might have wrecks.

5. The railroad property otherwise unhandled would disintegrate.

6. He would have a low volume of product.

7. His product would be uneven and bad as he could maintain no schedule.

8. There would shortly be no railroad.

Now let's "solve" this as it has been done in the past.

Let's appoint a person for each station and say "There we are!"

Well, it would still be a mess.

So let's hire more engineers and more station agents and more engineers and more station agents... and wind up with a confused mess, a huge payroll and a lousy product. That's how governments do it. And it is notable that current governments have no product but disaster.

No, we have to solve this in quite another way.

We do not get anywhere and we will not get a sensible org board and nothing will work or be viable unless WE COUNT THE PRODUCTS CORRECTLY AND DEVELOP HATS TO ATTAIN THEM.

When we have done this we can arrange the hats on an org board so there is a *flow* and command channels and communication channels and we've got an org board.

You cannot work out an org board until you have counted products!

As volume increases you estimate the products before the final product and hat those.

Quality of final product depends on a real org board and hats, both complete, real and trained-in and the functions DONE.

Let us see now how you break down a *final* product into the products which, put together, comprise it.

We have the final product of a railroad—viably moved loads. How many lesser products go into the big product?

There is a matter of machinery here. Any machine has two products: (a) the machine itself in good operating condition, (b) the product of the machine. A repairman and machine shop man and a repair shop keeper each has a product under (a). That is just for the machine, the engine.

Under (b) we have what the machine itself produces (hauled trains in the case of an engine).

Here we have then two major products—and these break down into lesser products, earlier in sequence to the final product.

There is even an earlier product to these—bought engines. And an earlier product to that—finance for equipment.

As for the load itself, a delivered load, accepted at the receiving end by a consignee, as you back up the sequence you will find a product—stored freight. And before that—unloaded freight. And before that—moved freight. And before that—loaded freight. And before that—freight assembled for shipment. And before that—freight contracts procured. And before that— advertising placed in public view. And before that—surveys of public freight requirement. And before that—survey for activities requiring freight service.

Each one of these products is a hat.

Surveying this again we see there's no charges or income involved so no economic viability. Thus there is an additional product, the income which is necessary for the organization's survival to pay its bills, buy the wherewithal necessary for future production and so on. This product has earlier hats of course. Some people (and a lot of executives) aren't product-minded—they think income falls into a company's lap or out of a TV set. They can't think the product sequence necessary to obtain income. So they go broke and starve. There are always a lot of prior products to the product of income. Fixated people just fixate on money itself, have no product sequence and so go broke or are poor.

Someone has to have a desirable product that is sold for more than it costs to produce and has to sell it and deliver it to have income.

Even in socialism or communism the how-does-it-support-itself question must be understood, answered, its product sequence identified, org boarded and hatted. In such a moneyless society the org boarding has to be much tighter as money adds flexibility and lack of it as a working factor makes problems that are hard to solve.

Organizing

In order to organize something one only has to:

1. Establish what is the final product.

2. Work backwards in sequence to establish the earlier products necessary to make each next product and which all in a row add up to the final product.

Ingredients delivered to bakery

Delivered ingredients

Prepped ingredients

Mixed ingredients

Kneaded ingredients

Baked bread

Packaged bread (final product)

3. Post it in terms of vertical greater and greater completeness of product to get command channels.

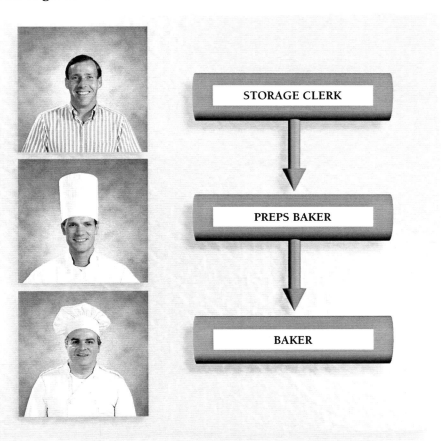

4. Adjust it for flows.

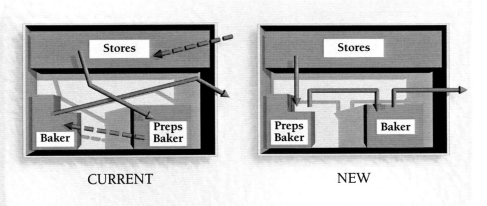

CURRENT   NEW

5. Assign its communication sequence.

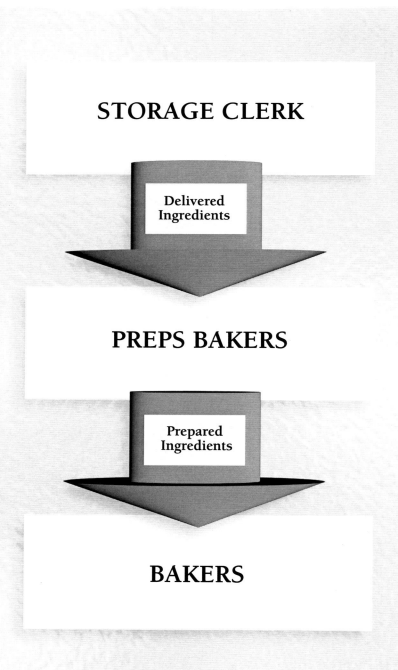

STORAGE CLERK

Delivered Ingredients

PREPS BAKERS

Prepared Ingredients

BAKERS

6. Work out the doing resulting in each product. Write these as functions and actions with all skills included.

BAKERY
FUNCTIONS AND ACTIONS

A.   Stocks of ingredients ready for delivery to
     Preps Bakers.

     Locate suppliers
     Purchase ingredients
     Store ingredients
     Handle accounting

B.   Ingredients prepared for Bakers in proper
     amounts.

     Read recipes
     Measure ingredients

C.   Ingredients mixed according to recipe, baked
     and decorated as needed.

     Read recipes
     Mixing ingredients
     Kneading dough
     Preparing pans
     Setting ovens
     Decorating items

7. Name these as posts.

BAKER

PREPS BAKER

STORAGE CLERK

8. Post it.

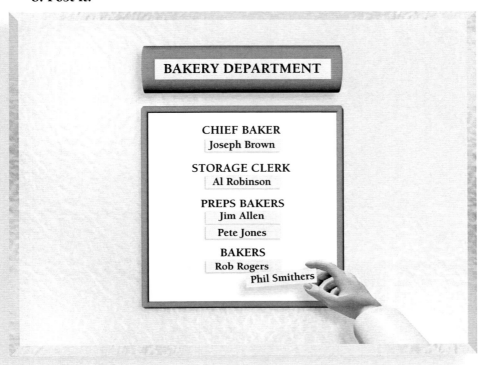

BAKERY DEPARTMENT

CHIEF BAKER
Joseph Brown

STORAGE CLERK
Al Robinson

PREPS BAKERS
Jim Allen

Pete Jones

BAKERS
Rob Rogers

Phil Smithers

9. Drill it to get it known.

Bakery Organizing Board

10. Assemble and issue packs of materials which describe the functions and duties of each hat.

11. Get these known.

12. Get the functions done so that the products occur.

The final product results when each of the prior steps in an organized activity is done.

This is what is called "organizing."

As a comment, because railroads *didn't* fully organize, their viability decayed and they ceased to be so used.

Railroads think it's the government or airplane rivalry or many other things. It isn't. They had too many missing hats, were actually too disorganized to keep pace with the society's demands, ceased to fully deliver and declined. In fact there has never been a greater need of railroads than today. Yet, disorganized, badly org boarded and hatted, they do not furnish the service they should and so are opposed, government regulated, union hammered and caved in.

To have a quality product, organize!

To raise morale, organize!

To survive, organize!

ORGANIZING BOARD

As you have read in the previous sections of this booklet, considerable breakthroughs were made in Scientology on the subject of organizing. However, these are but a small portion of the natural laws of organization discovered and developed in Scientology during research into and discovery of the fundamental axioms of all life. With the statement of these axioms—the basics of existence itself—light was cast upon all fields.

Scientology makes the able more able. Each of its organizations has the purpose to deliver this technology to the individuals of its community so they become more able, improve their lives and the lives of those around them. As a result, the individual can accomplish his personal goals, the community as a whole grows and a new civilization free from the insanity, conflict and strife that has plagued man for millennia will be created. Ultimately, this is the aim of Scientology.

To make it possible to maximally service individuals and its community, it is necessary for a Scientology organization to be highly organized and efficient. Existing organizational charts were typically only command charts that showed the direction of orders from the top down, and were far from usable for the unique purposes of a Scientology organization. Needed was an organizational pattern that primarily revolved around the delivery of Scientology services and provided the other functions necessary to not only continue the organization's existence but enable it to effortlessly expand while achieving its aims. Hence, it was necessary to formulate an organizing board particularly for Scientology organizations.

Each area of a Scientology organization functions in one of two ways. Either it delivers the services the organization offers, such as its many courses, or it assists these areas by hiring and placing personnel, paying the organization's bills, caring for its staff, informing public of the services the organization offers and many, many other activities. All of the portions of a Scientology organization operate together as a unified and dedicated whole to accomplish the organization's purpose. And it is the organizing board which provides it with the vital organizational foundation to bring about success.

Though originally developed for use by Scientology organizations, the beauty of this organizing board is its flexibility in application. Based as it is on the laws of life themselves, it can be applied to any area of endeavor and by any organization, no matter its function or size; furthermore, it can even be used by an individual to organize his own life and improve his own existence.

The organizing board is divided into seven distinct areas called *divisions*. These are numbered 1 through 7. Each one performs the functions necessary to produce a product specific to that division.

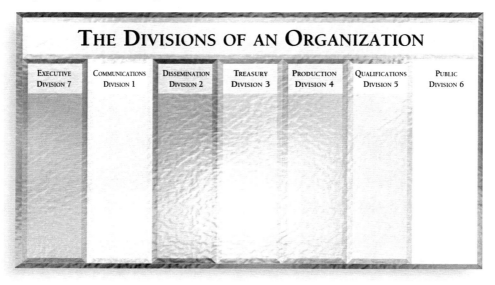

THE DIVISIONS OF AN ORGANIZATION

EXECUTIVE DIVISION 7	COMMUNICATIONS DIVISION 1	DISSEMINATION DIVISION 2	TREASURY DIVISION 3	PRODUCTION DIVISION 4	QUALIFICATIONS DIVISION 5	PUBLIC DIVISION 6

For any organization to be successful, all of the activities covered by these division names must be performed. These are: Executive, Communications, Dissemination (promoting and marketing of the organization's services and products), Treasury, Production, Qualifications (ensuring the quality of the organization's services and products), and Public (informing new public of the organization's services and products). An organization lacking one or more of these divisions will fail.

Although the seven division organizing board seems to have a number of divisions that would fit only a large group, it does, as mentioned, fit any organization of any size. The problem presented in deriving this board was how to overcome continual organizational changes because of expansion and how to apply it to organizations of different sizes. Thus this board goes from one person to thousands without change. Just fewer or more posts are occupied. That is the only change.

Unique to this organizing board is that it is entered from the left and proceeds to the right, starting with Division 1 and moving on through the divisions to Division 6, and then out. An individual or particle does not flow through Division 7—this division coordinates the activities of the rest of the organization and sees that it properly functions to accomplish its purpose. This organizing board would ideally be mounted on a large cylinder to show that it flows in a continuous circle with Division 7 meeting Division 1. To emphasize this fact, Division 7 is placed before the rest of the divisions on the board.

Divisions 1 through 7 are not arbitrarily arranged but describe a sequence known as the cycle of production. A fundamental law of this universe is that for any cycle of action to successfully complete, it must go through these exact seven main stages. In other words, for an organization or company to produce a high-quality product or service, it has to have all seven divisions properly operating. Down through the ages, innumerable civilizations, governments and groups fell prey to various ills and vanished from the face of the earth. It was a lack of one or more of these seven divisions that brought about these failures.

The direct application of this org board to an organization of any size or an individual's life is immediately evident upon inspection of it.

For instance, you would have to be in *Communication* with people about what you are doing and have your communication lines established.

Dissemination would involve telling people what you are producing, and promoting this.

You must have the physical materials to produce your product, which is *Treasury.* This includes funds to buy the materials and methods of purchasing them, as well as care for your assets.

Then there is *Production* of the product—the service being provided or item being produced.

And when the product is complete, *Qualifications* reviews it to make sure it meets the requirements of a product and if not, straightens out those involved so the product is valuable and can be exchanged. Qualifications also includes the furthering of your own education and training and that of an organization's personnel.

Once the product is qualified, the *Public* Division distributes it, creates new public who can obtain it and makes you and your products known to and desired by them.

Establishing goals and planning for the future is cared for by the *Executive* Division, which also keeps things operating and solves the various problems and bugs that may occur.

The functions performed by each division are further subdivided into *departments,* usually three in number, making twenty-one in total. Each department has a specific product or products which, when added together, result in the overall product of the division.

In a Communications Division, for example, the final product is effective, productive and ethical personnel. The first department is the Department of Routing and Personnel, which has a product of effective personnel posted and hatted. Some functions of this department are: receives individuals entering the organization and routes them to the correct terminal in the organization; hires personnel; determines the proper utilization of new staff and correctly places them to assist the organization's expansion; and sees that the organization's staff know their duties.

The Department of Communications is fully responsible for the communications into and out of the organization, as well as those which flow between organizational staff members. Its product is communications easily accepted and swiftly delivered. It answers the phones, swiftly directs calls to the correct terminal; receives incoming mail and swiftly distributes it to the staff throughout the organization; sees to it that the organization is communicating to its public in volume; establishes the organization's communications systems so its staff and executives can send and receive the communications necessary for the organization to successfully operate; and swiftly routes the internal despatches amongst the staff.

The Department of Inspections and Reports, with the product of ethical, producing personnel, is the third department. It inspects ongoing organizational projects and reports on their status to executives so, where needed, action can be taken to rectify any shortcomings; it collects and graphs the organization's statistics so these can be inspected and analyzed by its

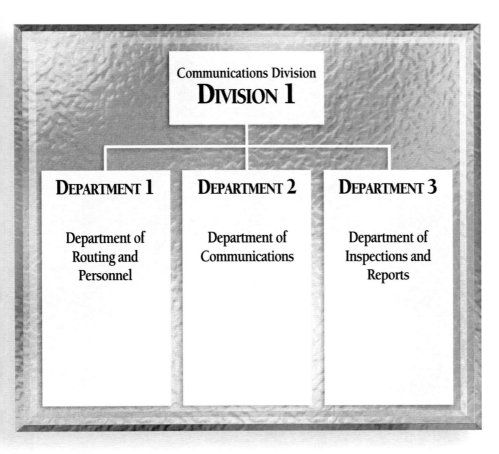

Communications Division
DIVISION 1

DEPARTMENT 1

Department of
Routing and
Personnel

DEPARTMENT 2

Department of
Communications

DEPARTMENT 3

Department of
Inspections and
Reports

executives to improve production and effectiveness; and maintains a high level of ethical behavior in the organization.

Every individual has his twenty-one department org board. The degree to which the functions of these departments are being performed regulates his survival and success.

Applying the organizing board to one's life is quite simple. By taking up the functions done by one department and comparing these to one's own activities, he can determine if these are being done or are missing. Continuing in this fashion for the remaining departments enables one to assess what functions or even departments are missing on his own org board. He can then take action to remedy these deficiencies and improve his life.

A simplified version of the Scientology org board follows. It describes the functions of the divisions as they can be applied by any individual, organization or group.

SEVEN DIVISION ORGANIZING BOARD

Any organization requires an executive structure that provides supervision and coordination of the divisions' activities. On this seven division organizing board, each division is headed by a secretary. To provide optimum guidance to the divisions, there are two Executive Secretaries. One supplies direction to three divisions; the other, four divisions. The entire organization is headed by an Executive Director. He works with and through the Executive Secretaries to see to the production and expansion of his organization.

COMMUNICATIONS EXECUTIVE SECRETARY

EXECUTIVE DIVISION
DIVISION 7
DIVISION 7 SECRETARY

OFFICE OF SOURCE	OFFICE OF EXTERNAL AFFAIRS	OFFICE OF THE EXECUTIVE DIRECTOR

This division coordinates and supervises the organization's activities so it runs smoothly, produces its products viably and delivers its products and services to individuals and the community in high quality.

OFFICE OF SOURCE
■ Sees to it that the technology and policy of the organization is followed without deviation. In the case of a company, this office could include the office of the person who started the organization or the one who had developed the product produced by the company. Keeps the organization's premises in good repair and acquires additional space to accommodate expansion.

OFFICE OF EXTERNAL AFFAIRS
■ Handles the external environment of the organization. Maintains proper governmental relations and cares for legal affairs.

OFFICE OF THE EXECUTIVE DIRECTOR
■ Does the organization's planning. Coordinates and gets the functions of the organization done. Keeps the organization solvent, viable, producing and expanding in all its divisions and departments.

COMMUNICATIONS DIVISION
DIVISION 1
COMMUNICATIONS SECRETARY

DEPARTMENT OF ROUTING AND PERSONNEL	DEPARTMENT OF COMMUNICATIONS	DEPARTMENT OF INSPECTIONS AND REPORTS

This division is fully responsible for the establishment of the organization.

DEPARTMENT OF ROUTING AND PERSONNEL
■ Hires eligible staff and properly places them for the benefit of the individual and the organization. Gets new and existing staff hatted and apprenticed to do their jobs.

DEPARTMENT OF COMMUNICATIONS
■ Sets up standard communications systems and gets in established communication routes so all communications are swiftly and properly handled. Makes sure that correspondence to and from the organization's public arrives and is swiftly handled.

DEPARTMENT OF INSPECTIONS AND REPORTS
■ Collects and accurately graphs the organization's statistics for executive use. Maintains a high level of ethical behavior among the staff. Inspects the organization's activities so any difficulties inhibiting expansion are detected and reported upon to the proper executive for swift resolution.

DISSEMINATION DIVISION
DIVISION 2
DISSEMINATION SECRETARY

DEPARTMENT OF PROMOTION AND MARKETING	DEPARTMENT OF PUBLICATIONS	DEPARTMENT OF REGISTRATION

This division makes the organization's products and services widely known and demanded, creating a high volume of public obtaining them.

DEPARTMENT OF PROMOTION AND MARKETING
■ Does informative mailings, magazines and other promotion based on survey results, to inform the public of the organization's services and products and the published materials it offers so these are acquired in a viable quantity.

DEPARTMENT OF PUBLICATIONS
■ Stocks all published materials so they are readily available for sale, and swiftly delivers these to individuals who purchase them.

DEPARTMENT OF REGISTRATION
■ Contacts individuals who have expressed interest in the organization's products so these are obtained by them. Keeps accurate files of people who previously received service or obtained products from the organization and maintains correspondence with them so they can acquire further products and services.

EXECUTIVE DIRECTOR

ORGANIZATION EXECUTIVE SECRETARY

TREASURY DIVISION
DIVISION 3
TREASURY SECRETARY

DEPARTMENT OF INCOME	DEPARTMENT OF DISBURSEMENTS	DEPARTMENT OF RECORDS, ASSETS AND MATERIEL

This division handles the financial matters, assets and materiel of the organization so its physical body is fully cared for, enabling it to produce its products and deliver its services and remain solvent.

DEPARTMENT OF INCOME
■ Handles incoming funds received in exchange for the organization's products so these are properly recorded. Accurately maintains customer accounts folders and collects all credit owed to the organization.

DEPARTMENT OF DISBURSEMENTS
■ Disburses funds for purchasing and the payment of all bills, as well as pays the staff, so its financial obligations are fulfilled and the other divisions have the wherewithal to produce their products.

DEPARTMENT OF RECORDS, ASSETS AND MATERIEL
■ Handles the organization's supplies, keeps precise records of all financial transactions, does necessary bookkeeping and financial reports and preserves assets and reserves.

PRODUCTION DIVISION
DIVISION 4
PRODUCTION SECRETARY

DEPARTMENT OF PRODUCTION SERVICES	DEPARTMENT OF ACTIVITY	DEPARTMENT OF PRODUCTION

This division provides excellent quality products and services with no delay to its public.

DEPARTMENT OF PRODUCTION SERVICES
■ Serves the division by prediction of what wherewithal is needed to produce and sees to its timely arrival so production can be done, and schedules production for maximum efficiency and service to the public.

DEPARTMENT OF ACTIVITY
■ Prepares the resources needed to produce the organization's products and deliver them.

DEPARTMENT OF PRODUCTION
■ Produces the organization's product and delivers its services rapidly, in high quantity and with excellent quality so people are satisfied with results.

QUALIFICATIONS DIVISION
DIVISION 5
QUALIFICATIONS SECRETARY

DEPARTMENT OF EXAMINATIONS	DEPARTMENT OF REVIEW	DEPARTMENT OF CERTIFICATIONS AND AWARDS

This division sees that every product leaving the organization has the expected level of quality.

DEPARTMENT OF EXAMINATIONS
■ Examines the validity and correctness of products, passing these to Review or Certification so every product is certified, or corrected so it can be certified.

DEPARTMENT OF REVIEW
■ Reviews the organization's product to isolate the causes for any lower-than-acceptable level of quality. Also reviews staff actions and corrects them where needed so technology and policy are applied with superb results. Cares for the staff as individuals so they become fully trained in all aspects of their jobs and organizational policy and technology and become competent, contributing group members.

DEPARTMENT OF CERTIFICATIONS AND AWARDS
■ Issues and records valid attestations of skill, state and merit honestly deserved, attained and earned. Observes for any flubbed products and ensures they are corrected.

PUBLIC DIVISION
DIVISION 6
PUBLIC SECRETARY

DEPARTMENT OF PUBLIC INFORMATION	DEPARTMENT OF CLEARING	DEPARTMENT OF SUCCESS

This division, through all of its activities, brings knowledge of and distributes the organization's services and products to the broad public.

DEPARTMENT OF PUBLIC INFORMATION
■ Sees to it that the appearance of the organization and its personnel is excellent. Makes the organization and its services and products well known to the community. Works with community groups and other organizations to improve the society.

DEPARTMENT OF CLEARING
■ Establishes and makes productive distribution points outside the organization which offer its services and products to new public.

DEPARTMENT OF SUCCESS
■ Records and makes widely known to the public the successes of the organization's activities and its products.

ORGANIZING AND MORALE

The basics of organizing as found in this booklet present discoveries that can reverse the decline of any organization and bring about productivity or increase the orderly expansion of an already thriving group. They can be utilized in the home, school or the workplace—the scope of application is limitless. An individual can benefit by organizing his activities.

If you organize well and efficiently, you will have good morale. You will also have improved conditions.

Wherever morale is bad, organize!

A very careful survey of people shows that their basic protests are against lack of organization. "It doesn't run right!" is the reason they protest things.

Applying the organizing technology can smooth over these protests, bringing about increased production and thus better morale.

While they may necessitate some change in methods of operation for the individual or group, these basics of organizing are relatively simple to apply. And if success is desirable, they are well worth the effort, for they have been conclusively proven to work. By utilizing these principles any endeavor can be made to flourish.■

PRACTICAL EXERCISES

1 Write down something you want to accomplish; e.g., a clean car, a small garden planted, a room in one's house repainted, etc. This should be something that you could do in the present and in a relatively short amount of time. Then list out the series of actions that would be done to accomplish the final completion of this action. Repeat the above two more times for different things you want to accomplish.

2 Take one of the lists you wrote out in the previous exercise and actually carry the steps out to the completion of the action.

3 Write down a product of an organization or activity with which you have some familiarity. Then write down how this product is exchanged inside or outside the organization or activity.

4 Do the following steps:

a. Write down the name of a post or job with which you have some familiarity.

b. Write down the particle or particles that would be handled by this post or job.

c. Write down how the particle(s) you listed in step (b) would be changed by a person holding the job or post.

d. Repeat steps (a) to (c) for two other examples of posts or jobs.

5 Briefly describe your own hat, and write down its product(s). Repeat these two steps ten more times for other hats in organizations or activities of which you have some knowledge.

6 For one of the hats you named in the previous exercise, write a list of contents that would be included in the pack of materials that would teach an individual the actions to produce the product of the job. Do this for one other hat from the same list.

7 Do the following steps:

a. Work out and write down the final product of an organization, part of an organization or an activity with which you have some familiarity.

b. Figure out and list the lesser products earlier in sequence to the final product, working backwards in sequence.

c. Write down how you would post it to get command channels.

d. Repeat steps (a)–(c) for two other organizations or activities that you have familiarity or knowledge of.

8 Write down the name of an activity, organization or part of an organization you have observed or been part of which had flows in need of adjustment. Draw out as best you can what the existing flows are. Then draw out how the flows should be adjusted to improve its organization and production.

9 Pick one of the lesser products you listed in #7 above. Write down three examples of the functions and actions that would be done to bring about that lesser product. Repeat this for two other lesser products.

10 Using the data you wrote up in Exercise #7, write down for yourself three examples of posts that would do the functions to bring about the lesser products and final products.

11 With the data in the previous two practicals and in Exercise #7, work out the organization's or activity's Production Division. Refer to the materials in this booklet to carry out the steps necessary to do this. Sketch out the Production Division, showing the different posts by name.

12 Write down a realistic example of an action you could do that would be part of the Communications Division in an organization or activity. Repeat this for each of the remaining six divisions: Dissemination, Treasury, Production, Qualifications, Public and Executive.

13 Get a large piece of paper, or tape several sheets together to make a large sheet of paper. Using the seven division organizing board given in this book, sketch out an outline of a twenty-one department organizing board. Do this as follows: (a) Lay the paper on a flat surface, turned in such a way that the long length is lying from left to right in front of you. (b) Draw vertical dividing lines for the seven divisions. Use up the whole width of your paper except for small margins on each side. Each division is to be approximately the same width, equally spaced across the paper. Draw horizontal lines across the top and bottom of the vertical lines you drew. Leave about five inches of space at the top of the page. (c) Draw in the three departments for each division, each department approximately the same width. (d) Write in the names of the divisions and departments along the top of each in the sketch. Go on to the next exercise.

14 As the final exercise, work out a twenty-one department org board for your own life. To do this, use the twenty-one department org board outline you drew in the previous exercise and the seven division organizing board on pages 34–35. Compare your life to the functions of the divisions and departments to locate those which are missing. Take up the functions given for Department 1 and determine which are being performed in your life and which are not. Where you find one is missing (not being performed in your life), write it down in the Department 1 column on your org board outline. Then go on to the next department. Continue in this fashion until you have analyzed your life against the entire organizing board. Utilize what you found in this analysis to get in the missing functions and departments in your life.

RESULTS FROM APPLICATION

Dramatic and lasting changes have been made by individuals, family members and executives through using the basic tools of organizing as formulated by Mr. Hubbard. Organizing technology left the dark ages forever with the discoveries he made. The ease and effectiveness of application create daily miracles in the companies and corporations of those who use them. Its application in the home has made for much more fulfilling and productive familial activities. Business stress and its accompanying array of illnesses become a thing of the past replaced by well-being and a true enjoyment of production. This technology even combats the unpredictability of future survival for oneself and one's group endeavors. The resultant raised productivity and satisfaction gained from being able to causatively direct the course of organizational affairs is reflected in the accounts of application below.

As the president of an environmental company in Burbank, California, a man has used L. Ron Hubbard's administrative technology for the entire twelve years the company has been operating.

"We have grown from one small office with an individual founder to a 26,000-square-foot corporate headquarters with two hundred staff and ten offices throughout California. Our company has been listed for three years in a row in the top five hundred fastest growing private corporations in the United States. This is a direct result of L. Ron Hubbard's administrative technology on organizing boards and other subjects, all designed to get results. After majoring in business at Illinois University, I knew very little about the actual operation of a company. I can attribute the success of this company to the use of Mr. Hubbard's technology and to that alone."

A young sailor had the goal to work in the music industry. He worked on this but didn't really get anywhere until he became familiar with Mr. Hubbard's technology on organizing boards:

"I had been dealing with professional music all my life before I became a sailor and wanted to go back to work with music. I really tried to make it happen, but this had been going on for the better part of five years with no result. Then I learned about Mr. Hubbard's technology concerning org

PROVEN WORKABILITY

While a 10 percent annual expansion rate is very acceptable to many companies, those who use Scientology administrative principles routinely achieve a far higher degree of success.

25% TO 200%

10%

Expansion rate considered successful

Expansion rates with use of Scientology administrative technology boards and started applying specifically the data on Divisions 4 and 6. I suddenly found my skills in demand. Less than a month after beginning to apply this data, I was approached by a personnel director from a music company who wanted me to start working in a very advanced music studio. While waiting to get started, I got into production as a music composer and continued my personal promotion. I was hired and am now where I want to be. The turning point for all this was without doubt the application of the technology about org boards. Doing this made everything fall into place."

An executive in Washington, DC was put in charge of a major operation and luckily knew Mr. Hubbard's technology about organizing. She applied it and got the following result:

"By using L. Ron Hubbard's technology on organizing I was able to get a unit of twenty-five people organized up with lines and terminals and getting out products on a twenty-four-hour basis. (This was an unusual situation where the night crew had to prepare materials throughout the night and have them ready to go for the day crew each morning by 7 A.M.) I used the exact data on organizing, followed it to the letter and drilled the crew on everything. It took me a day or two to prepare the drilling but once it was applied, the whole thing worked like magic. The drilled crew was there, knew exactly what to do, what their other team members were doing, and it went off like clockwork."

A young woman's experience with organizing an activity demonstrated to her the value of Mr. Hubbard's organizational principles:

"Some time ago I went with fifteen other people to do a major convention in Florida, in which we had over two hundred people receiving services. We were not organized properly at all, had not given specific hats to each person and so were stumbling over each other, had complaints about slow service, and were running ourselves into the ground trying to keep track of everything. We didn't want to repeat our errors at the next convention we did in England, and so we decided to learn something from our earlier mistakes. We worked out a simple org board for the upcoming convention detailing who was going to take care of what functions and assigned specific hats to the people who were there. The result? We serviced several hundred people with less personnel and had far less confusion than the first convention. This couldn't have been accomplished had we not used Mr. Hubbard's technology on organizing boards."

An Australian carpenter was hired by a carpentry shop that did both general woodworking and furniture manufacturing. They had a large contract coming up to produce all of the furniture needed for a huge apartment complex but they were not set up for efficient production.

"About six months ago I was given a job in a carpentry shop. When I first arrived in the area I didn't know where anything was and oddly enough neither did the other carpenters. There was a lot of upset about tools going missing and someone working over the top of someone else's project. This situation created a lot of confusion and slowed production.

"The department head put me on a project to set up the shop so real production could occur. I had been studying Mr. Hubbard's

Administrative Technology and jumped at the opportunity to put it to use in a big way.

"The first thing I did was set up work stations for each carpenter. These included his tools and anything he would need to produce a product.

"I then worked out the lines that were needed to take a piece of furniture from rough wood through to a finished product, and put these lines in.

"With all the lines in and each carpenter's area set up there is no longer any upset over missing tools or overdue products. Things get done on time and everyone in the shop takes pride in keeping in a high quality standard."

Analyzing her own life against the organizing board helped a California artist regain a bright outlook for the future and start doing what she needed to do to make that future a reality:

"I've realized that working out my personal organizing board is making confusion blow off and order come into my life! I feel like a STAR! My abilities are opening up and all this is effortless, painless and very direct. Evaluating my life this way is a wonderful experience. No feeling of wrongness, blame or guilt attached. I am becoming more aware and can see myself going on a continuous 'up' from here. I'm HAPPY!"

A large construction site was not fully productive. Several urgently needed buildings were seriously behind schedule and with the existing organization the needed production was not occurring. The French construction manager, who had studied

Mr. Hubbard's organizational data, reorganized the area using what he had learned.

"Looking over the existing scene it became evident that our production units were not properly organized.

"My company specializes in construction of buildings and spans across all trades involved in the development of a building.

"Based on Mr. Hubbard's technology of the organizing board, all functions needed to build a building were isolated and named. The flows between each function were also worked out. Based on this it was then possible to group similar activities and to form up units and sections.

"Hats were assigned and all personnel were posted on the new org board and hatted and drilled on their new posts.

"Statistics were worked out which measure actual production and enforce post responsibility.

"The result of this rudimentary reorganization was a definite increase in production with products flowing across each post. Furthermore each of my crew has become a tradesman and artisan and each product produced is achieved with great pride."

A German kindergarten teacher found that small children take delight in having a post on the org board and in learning new skills.

"I studied L. Ron Hubbard's data on organization and used it to organize my life. As a result I get a lot more things done; I use the data in all areas of my life, in my family, in my own time and on the job.

"I was working with children in our kindergarten and used this data with them; they each had their own posts and were

responsible for getting them done. They were also trained in **how** to do their posts with lots of practical drilling until they felt sure they could do it. Each one of them told me what he wanted to do and what he would like to know and to learn. They felt very proud about their new skills and wanted to learn more and more.

"They had their own org board, and when someone needed something to be done, they knew who to see for this. When there were mistakes, they got corrected in the Qualifications Division. We made our own financial plans for the week and figured out what we wanted to buy for the money we had. They also began to make sure that everybody did the job he was responsible for, and as a result we had much more time to play. They absolutely loved it and it was great to see how they handled their areas and other persons; children as well as adults.

"This group was so well organized that I could take six three-year-olds to the department store or the underground and none of them would do anything unpredictable.

"I was often asked by people observing this how I managed to do it. It seemed to be impossible but it was actually very easy to do with the application of L. Ron Hubbard's data on organization."

GLOSSARY

beingness: condition or state of being; existence. *Beingness* also refers to the assumption or choosing of a category of identity. Beingness can be assumed by oneself or given to oneself or attained. Examples of beingness would be one's own name, one's profession, one's physical characteristics, one's role in a game—each or all of these could be called one's beingness.

communication: an interchange of ideas across space between two individuals.

communication line: the route along which a communication travels from one person to another.

cycle of action: the sequence that an action goes through, wherein the action is begun, is continued for as long as is required and then is completed as planned.

doingness: the performance of some action or activity.

hat: *(slang)* the title and work of a post in an organization. It is taken from the fact that in many professions such as railroading the type of hat worn is the badge of the job. For example, a train crew has a conductor who wears a conductor's hat—he has charge of the passengers and collects fares. To *hat* someone is to train him on the functions and specialties of his post, and when a person is fully trained to do these he is said to be *hatted*.

org board: short for *organizing board*, a board which displays the functions, duties, communication routes, sequences of action and authorities of an organization. It shows the pattern of organizing to obtain a product.

Scientology: an applied religious philosophy developed by L. Ron Hubbard. It is the study and handling of the spirit in relationship to itself, universes and other life. The word *Scientology* comes from the Latin *scio,* which means "know" and the Greek word *logos,* meaning "the word or outward form by which the inward thought is expressed and made known." Thus, Scientology means knowing about knowing.

terminal: a person, point or position which can receive, relay or send a communication.

ABOUT L. RON HUBBARD

Born in Tilden, Nebraska on March 13, 1911, his road of discovery and dedication to his fellows began at an early age. By the age of nineteen, he had traveled more than a quarter of a million miles, examining the cultures of Java, Japan, India and the Philippines.

Returning to the United States in 1929, Ron resumed his formal education and studied mathematics, engineering and the then new field of nuclear physics—all providing vital tools for continued research. To finance that research, Ron embarked upon a literary career in the early 1930s, and soon became one of the most widely read authors of popular fiction. Yet never losing sight of his primary goal, he continued his mainline research through extensive travel and expeditions.

With the advent of World War II, he entered the United States Navy as a lieutenant (junior grade) and served as commander of antisubmarine corvettes. Left partially blind and lame from injuries sustained during combat, he was diagnosed as permanently disabled by 1945. Through application of his theories on the mind, however, he was not only able to help fellow servicemen, but also to regain his own health.

After five more years of intensive research, Ron's discoveries were presented to the world in *Dianetics: The Modern Science of Mental Health*. The first popular handbook on the human mind expressly written for the man in the street, *Dianetics* ushered in a new era of hope for mankind and a new phase of life for its author. He did, however, not cease his research, and as breakthrough after breakthrough was carefully codified through late 1951, the applied religious philosophy of Scientology was born.

Because Scientology explains the whole of life, there is no aspect of man's existence that L. Ron Hubbard's subsequent work did not address. Residing variously in the United States and England, his continued research brought forth solutions to such social ills as declining educational standards and pandemic drug abuse.

All told, L. Ron Hubbard's works on Scientology and Dianetics total forty million words of recorded lectures, books and writings. Together, these constitute the legacy of a lifetime that ended on January 24, 1986. Yet the passing of L. Ron Hubbard in no way constituted an end; for with a hundred million of his books in circulation and millions of people daily applying his technologies for betterment, it can truly be said the world still has no greater friend. ■

CHURCHES OF SCIENTOLOGY
Contact Your Nearest Church or Organization or visit www.volunteerministers.org

UNITED STATES

ALBUQUERQUE
Church of Scientology
8106 Menaul Boulevard NE
Albuquerque, New Mexico
87110

ANN ARBOR
Church of Scientology
66 E. Michigan Avenue
Battle Creek, Michigan 49017

ATLANTA
Church of Scientology
1611 Mt. Vernon Road
Dunwoody, Georgia 30338

AUSTIN
Church of Scientology
2200 Guadalupe
Austin, Texas 78705

BOSTON
Church of Scientology
448 Beacon Street
Boston, Massachusetts 02115

BUFFALO
Church of Scientology
47 West Huron Street
Buffalo, New York 14202

CHICAGO
Church of Scientology
3011 North Lincoln Avenue
Chicago, Illinois 60657-4207

CINCINNATI
Church of Scientology
215 West 4th Street, 5th Floor
Cincinnati, Ohio 45202-2670

CLEARWATER
Church of Scientology
Flag Service Organization
210 South Fort Harrison Avenue
Clearwater, Florida 33756

Foundation Church of
  Scientology
Flag Ship Service Organization
c/o *Freewinds* Relay Office
118 North Fort Harrison Avenue
Clearwater, Florida 33755-4013

COLUMBUS
Church of Scientology
30 North High Street
Columbus, Ohio 43215

DALLAS
Church of Scientology
Celebrity Centre Dallas
1850 North Buckner Boulevard
Dallas, Texas 75228

DENVER
Church of Scientology
3385 South Bannock Street
Englewood, Colorado 80110

DETROIT
Church of Scientology
28000 Middlebelt Road
Farmington Hills, Michigan
48334

HONOLULU
Church of Scientology
1146 Bethel Street
Honolulu, Hawaii 96813

KANSAS CITY
Church of Scientology
3619 Broadway
Kansas City, Missouri 64111

LAS VEGAS
Church of Scientology
846 East Sahara Avenue
Las Vegas, Nevada 89104

Church of Scientology
Celebrity Centre Las Vegas
4850 W. Flamingo Road, Suite 10
Las Vegas, Nevada 89103

LONG ISLAND
Church of Scientology
99 Railroad Station Plaza
Hicksville, New York
11801-2850

LOS ANGELES AND VICINITY
Church of Scientology
  of Los Angeles
4810 Sunset Boulevard
Los Angeles, California 90027

Church of Scientology
1451 Irvine Boulevard
Tustin, California 92680

Church of Scientology
1277 East Colorado Boulevard
Pasadena, California 91106

Church of Scientology
15643 Sherman Way
Van Nuys, California 91406

Church of Scientology
American Saint Hill
  Organization
1413 L. Ron Hubbard Way
Los Angeles, California 90027

Church of Scientology
American Saint Hill Foundation
1413 L. Ron Hubbard Way
Los Angeles, California 90027

Church of Scientology
Advanced Organization
  of Los Angeles
1306 L. Ron Hubbard Way
Los Angeles, California 90027

Church of Scientology
Celebrity Centre International
5930 Franklin Avenue
Hollywood, California 90028

LOS GATOS
Church of Scientology
2155 South Bascom Avenue,
  Suite 120
Campbell, California 95008

MIAMI
Church of Scientology
120 Giralda Avenue
Coral Gables, Florida 33134

MINNEAPOLIS
Church of Scientology
Twin Cities
1011 Nicollet Mall
Minneapolis, Minnesota 55403

MOUNTAIN VIEW
Church of Scientology
2483 Old Middlefield Way
Mountain View, California
94043

NASHVILLE
Church of Scientology
Celebrity Centre Nashville
1204 16th Avenue South
Nashville, Tennessee 37212

NEW HAVEN
Church of Scientology
909 Whalley Avenue
New Haven, Connecticut
06515-1728

NEW YORK CITY
Church of Scientology
227 West 46th Street
New York, New York
10036-1409

Church of Scientology
Celebrity Centre New York
65 East 82nd Street
New York, New York 10028

ORLANDO
Church of Scientology
1830 East Colonial Drive
Orlando, Florida 32803-4729

PHILADELPHIA
Church of Scientology
1315 Race Street
Philadelphia, Pennsylvania
19107

PHOENIX
Church of Scientology
2111 West University Drive
Mesa, Arizona 85201

PORTLAND
Church of Scientology
2636 NE Sandy Boulevard
Portland, Oregon 97232-2342

Church of Scientology
Celebrity Centre Portland
708 SW Salmon Street
Portland, Oregon 97205

SACRAMENTO
Church of Scientology
825 15th Street
Sacramento, California
95814-2096

SALT LAKE CITY
Church of Scientology
1931 South 1100 East
Salt Lake City, Utah 84106

SAN DIEGO
Church of Scientology
1330 4th Avenue
San Diego, California 92101

SAN FRANCISCO
Church of Scientology
83 McAllister Street
San Francisco, California 9410[

SAN JOSE
Church of Scientology
80 East Rosemary Street
San Jose, California 95112

SANTA BARBARA
Church of Scientology
524 State Street
Santa Barbara, California 9310[

SEATTLE
Church of Scientology
2226 3rd Avenue
Seattle, Washington 98121

ST. LOUIS
Church of Scientology
6901 Delmar Boulevard
University City, Missouri 6313[

TAMPA
Church of Scientology
3617 Henderson Boulevard
Tampa, Florida 33609-4501

WASHINGTON, DC
Founding Church of Scientolo[
  of Washington, DC
1701 20th Street NW
Washington, DC 20009

PUERTO RICO

HATO REY
Dianetics Center of Puerto Ric[
272 JT Piñero Avenue
Hyde Park
San Juan, Puerto Rico 00918

CANADA

EDMONTON
Church of Scientology
10206 106th Street NW
Edmonton, Alberta
Canada T5J 1H7

ITCHENER
Church of Scientology
)4 King Street West, 2nd Floor
itchener, Ontario
anada N2G 1A6

IONTREAL
Church of Scientology
489 Papineau Street
ontreal, Quebec
anada H2H 1T7

OTTAWA
Church of Scientology
50 Rideau Street, 2nd Floor
ttawa, Ontario
anada K1N 5X6

QUEBEC
Church of Scientology
50 Bd Chareste Est
uebec, Quebec
anada G1K 3H5

ORONTO
Church of Scientology
96 Yonge Street, 2nd Floor
ronto, Ontario
anada M4Y 2A7

ANCOUVER
Church of Scientology
01 West Hastings Street
ancouver, British Columbia
anada V6B 1L5

VINNIPEG
Church of Scientology
15 Garry Street, Suite 210
innipeg, Manitoba
anada R3B 2G7

NITED KINGDOM

IRMINGHAM
Church of Scientology
Ethel Street
inston Churchill House
rmingham, England B2 4BG

RIGHTON
Church of Scientology
aird Floor, 79-83 North Street
ighton, Sussex
agland BN1 1ZA

AST GRINSTEAD
Church of Scientology
int Hill Foundation
int Hill Manor
ist Grinstead, West Sussex
agland RH19 4JY

lvanced Organization
Saint Hill
int Hill Manor
ist Grinstead, West Sussex
agland RH19 4JY

DINBURGH
ubbard Academy of Personal
Independence
Southbridge
linburgh, Scotland EH1 1LL

LONDON
Church of Scientology
68 Tottenham Court Road
London, England W1P 0BB

Church of Scientology
Celebrity Centre London
42 Leinster Gardens
London, England W2 3AN

MANCHESTER
Church of Scientology
258 Deansgate
Manchester, England M3 4BG

PLYMOUTH
Church of Scientology
41 Ebrington Street
Plymouth, Devon
England PL4 9AA

SUNDERLAND
Church of Scientology
51 Fawcett Street
Sunderland, Tyne and Wear
England SR1 1RS

AUSTRALIA

ADELAIDE
Church of Scientology
24–28 Waymouth Street
Adelaide, South Australia
Australia 5000

BRISBANE
Church of Scientology
106 Edward Street, 2nd Floor
Brisbane, Queensland
Australia 4000

CANBERRA
Church of Scientology
43–45 East Row
Canberra City, ACT
Australia 2601

MELBOURNE
Church of Scientology
42–44 Russell Street
Melbourne, Victoria
Australia 3000

PERTH
Church of Scientology
108 Murray Street, 1st Floor
Perth, Western Australia
Australia 6000

SYDNEY
Church of Scientology
201 Castlereagh Street
Sydney, New South Wales
Australia 2000

Church of Scientology
Advanced Organization
Saint Hill Australia,
New Zealand and Oceania
19–37 Greek Street
Glebe, New South Wales
Australia 2037

NEW ZEALAND

AUCKLAND
Church of Scientology
159 Queen Street, 3rd Floor
Auckland 1, New Zealand

AFRICA

BULAWAYO
Church of Scientology
Southampton House, Suite 202
Main Street and 9th Avenue
Bulawayo, Zimbabwe

CAPE TOWN
Church of Scientology
Ground Floor, Dorlane House
39 Roeland Street
Cape Town 8001, South Africa

DURBAN
Church of Scientology
20 Buckingham Terrace
Westville, Durban 3630
South Africa

HARARE
Church of Scientology
404-409 Pockets Building
50 Jason Moyo Avenue
Harare, Zimbabwe

JOHANNESBURG
Church of Scientology
4th Floor, Budget House
130 Main Street
Johannesburg 2001
South Africa

Church of Scientology
No. 108 1st Floor,
Bordeaux Centre
Gordon Road, Corner Jan
Smuts Avenue
Blairgowrie, Randburg 2125
South Africa

PORT ELIZABETH
Church of Scientology
2 St. Christopher's
27 Westbourne Road Central
Port Elizabeth 6001
South Africa

PRETORIA
Church of Scientology
307 Ancore Building
Corner Jeppe and Esselen Streets
Sunnyside, Pretoria 0002
South Africa

SCIENTOLOGY MISSIONS

INTERNATIONAL OFFICE
Scientology Missions
International
6331 Hollywood Boulevard
Suite 501
Los Angeles, California
90028-6314

UNITED STATES
Scientology Missions
International
Western United States Office
1308 L. Ron Hubbard Way
Los Angeles, California 90027

Scientology Missions
International
Eastern United States Office
349 W. 48th Street
New York, New York 10036

Scientology Missions
International
Flag Land Base Office
210 South Fort Harrison Avenue
Clearwater, Florida 33756

AFRICA
Scientology Missions
International
African Office
6th Floor, Budget House
130 Main Street
Johannesburg 2001
South Africa

AUSTRALIA, NEW ZEALAND AND OCEANIA
Scientology Missions
International
Australian, New Zealand
and Oceanian Office
201 Castlereagh Street, 3rd Flr.
Sydney, New South Wales
Australia 2000

CANADA
Scientology Missions
International
Canadian Office
696 Yonge Street
Toronto, Ontario
Canada M4Y 2A7

UNITED KINGDOM
Scientology Missions
International
United Kingdom Office
Saint Hill Manor
East Grinstead, West Sussex,
England RH19 4JY

TO OBTAIN ANY BOOKS OR CAS-
SETTES BY L. RON HUBBARD WHICH
ARE NOT AVAILABLE AT YOUR LOCAL
ORGANIZATION, CONTACT ANY OF
THE FOLLOWING PUBLICATIONS
ORGANIZATIONS WORLDWIDE:

BRIDGE PUBLICATIONS, INC.
4751 Fountain Avenue
Los Angeles, California 90029
www.bridgepub.com

NEW ERA PUBLICATIONS
INTERNATIONAL ApS
Store Kongensgade 53
1264 Copenhagen K
Denmark
www.newerapublications.com

BUILD A BETTER WORLD

BECOME A VOLUNTEER MINISTER

Help bring happiness, purpose and truth to your fellow man. Become a Volunteer Minister.

Thousands of Volunteer Ministers bring relief and sanity to others all over the world using techniques like the ones found in this booklet. But more help is needed. Your help. As a Volunteer Minister you can today handle things which seemed impossible yesterday. And you can vastly improve this world's tomorrow.

Become a Volunteer Minister and brighten the world to a better place for you to live. It's easy to do. For help and information about becoming a Volunteer Minister, visit our website today. www.volunteerministers.org

You can also call or write your nearest Volunteer Ministers International organization.

VOLUNTEER MINISTERS INTERNATIONAL

A DEPARTMENT OF THE INTERNATIONAL HUBBARD ECCLESIASTICAL LEAGUE OF PASTORS

INTERNATIONAL OFFICE
6331 Hollywood Boulevard, Suite 708
Los Angeles, California 90028
Tel: (323) 960-3560 (800) 435-7498

WESTERN US
1308 L. Ron Hubbard Way
Los Angeles, California 90027
Tel: (323) 953-3357
1-888-443-5760
ihelpwestus@earthlink.net

EASTERN US
349 W. 48th Street
New York, New York 10036
Tel: (212) 757-9610
1-888-443-5788

CANADA
696 Yonge Street
Toronto, Ontario
Canada M4Y 2A7
Tel: (416) 968-0070

LATIN AMERICA
Federación Mexicana de
Dianética, A.C.
Puebla #31
Colonia Roma, CP 06700
Mexico, D.F.
Tel: 525-511-4452

EUROPE
Store Kongensgade 55
1264 Copenhagen K
Denmark
Tel: 45-33-737-322

ITALY
Via Cadorna, 61
20090 Vimodrone (MI)
Italy
Tel: 39-0227-409-246

AUSTRALIA
201 Castlereagh Street
3rd Floor
Sydney, New South Wales
Australia 2000
Tel: 612-9267-6422

AFRICA
6th Floor, Budget House
130 Main Street
Johannesburg 2001
South Africa
Tel: 083-331-7170

UNITED KINGDOM
Saint Hill Manor
East Grinstead, West Sussex
England RH19 4JY
Tel: 44-1342-301-895

HUNGARY
1438 Budapest
PO Box 351, Hungary
Tel: 361-321-5298

COMMONWEALTH OF INDEPENDENT STATES
c/o Hubbard Humanitarian
Center
Ul. Borisa Galushkina 19A
129301 Moscow, Russia
Tel: 7-095-961-3414

TAIWAN
2F, 65, Sec. 4
Ming-Sheng East Road
Taipei, Taiwan ROC
Tel: 88-628-770-5074

www.volunteerministers.org

NEW ERA Publications International ApS
Store Kongensgade 53, 1264 Copenhagen K, Denmark
ISBN 87-7968-404-1

An L. RON HUBBARD Publication